2018 SQA Specimen and Past Papers with Answers

National 5
DESIGN AND MANUFACTURE

2017 & 2018 Exams
and 2017 Specimen Question Paper

Hodder Gibson Study Skills Advice –
  National 5 Design and Manufacture – page 3
Hodder Gibson Study Skills Advice – General – page 5
2017 EXAM – page 7
2017 SPECIMEN QUESTION PAPER – page 29
2018 EXAM – page 59
ANSWERS – page 81

HODDER GIBSON
AN HACHETTE UK COMPANY

This book contains the official SQA 2017 and 2018 Exams, and the 2017 Specimen Question Paper for National 5 Design and Manufacture, with associated SQA-approved answers modified from the official marking instructions that accompany the paper.

In addition the book contains study skills advice. This advice has been specially commissioned by Hodder Gibson, and has been written by experienced senior teachers and examiners in line with the new National 5 syllabus and assessment outlines. This is not SQA material but has been devised to provide further guidance for National 5 examinations.

Hodder Gibson is grateful to the copyright holders, as credited on the final page of the Answer section, for permission to use their material. Every effort has been made to trace the copyright holders and to obtain their permission for the use of copyright material. Hodder Gibson will be happy to receive information allowing us to rectify any error or omission in future editions.

Hachette UK's policy is to use papers that are natural, renewable and recyclable products and made from wood grown in sustainable forests. The logging and manufacturing processes are expected to conform to the environmental regulations of the country of origin.

Orders: please contact Bookpoint Ltd, 130 Park Drive, Milton Park, Abingdon, Oxon OX14 4SE. Telephone: (44) 01235 827827. Fax: (44) 01235 400454. Lines are open 9.00–5.00, Monday to Saturday, with a 24-hour message answering service. Visit our website at www.hoddereducation.co.uk. Hodder Gibson can also be contacted directly at hoddergibson@hodder.co.uk

This collection first published in 2018 by
Hodder Gibson, an imprint of Hodder Education,
An Hachette UK Company
211 St Vincent Street
Glasgow G2 5QY

National 5 2017 and 2018 Exam Papers and Answers; 2017 Specimen Question Paper and Answers © Scottish Qualifications Authority. Study Skills section © Hodder Gibson. All rights reserved. Apart from any use permitted under UK copyright law, no part of this publication may be reproduced or transmitted in any form or by any means, electronic or mechanical, including photocopying and recording, or held within any information storage and retrieval system, without permission in writing from the publisher or under licence from the Copyright Licensing Agency Limited. Further details of such licences (for reprographic reproduction) may be obtained from the Copyright Licensing Agency Limited, Saffron House, 6–10 Kirby Street, London EC1N 8TS.

Typeset by Aptara, Inc.

Printed in the UK

A catalogue record for this title is available from the British Library

ISBN: 978-1-5104-5659-4

2 1

2019 2018

Introduction

National 5 Design and Manufacture

This book of SQA past papers contains the question papers used in the 2017 and 2018 exams (with answers at the back of the book). A specimen question paper reflecting the content and duration of the exam in 2018 is also included.

All of the question papers included in the book provide excellent representative exam practice for the final exams. Using these papers as part of your revision will help you to develop the vital skills and techniques needed for the exam, and will help you identify any knowledge gaps you may have.

It is always a very good idea to refer to SQA's website for the most up-to-date course specification documents. These are available at www.sqa.org.uk/sqa/47457

The exam

The following guidance will give you a clear plan to take into the examination room and help you achieve better grades. The Design and Manufacture examination is split into two sections.

Section 1

Section 1 is worth 60 marks and is split into two equal (30 mark) areas of questioning. Question 1, which consists of 30 marks and is split into many sub-sections, is based around the workshop manufacturing techniques that could be used to manufacture a simple product. All the areas of questioning in this section will be about the product and its component parts. It is likely that there will be a mixture of materials used in the manufacture of the product. Those materials will most likely be wood, metal and plastic. A good examination preparation strategy would be to ensure you have knowledge of the properties of a range of softwoods, hardwoods, ferrous and non-ferrous metals, thermoplastics and thermosetting plastics. In addition, you will need to be familiar with common workshop processes using these materials. The tools and equipment used with these materials are also areas which you should study. Remember – none of this is new to you and you will have spent time on the Design and Manufacture course making a range of projects from these materials. Be confident.

The remaining questions in Section 1 are worth 30 marks and will ask mainly about the design section of the course; the context of the questions will be design work and products that focus on a specific aspect of design.

For the rest of the questions in this section, you should think back through your course and use the design tasks you experienced to assist you in formulating responses. This should help you answer the questions about the design process, sketching, modelling, specifications and other design related activities you were involved with.

The design questions will come from a range of topics which you will have covered in the course, such as the design team, the design process, design factors, sketching, modelling, product evaluation and specifications. A simple word can be used to help you remember the design factors: **FEEDSCAMP**

Each letter stands for one of the design factors: **F**unction, **E**rgonomics, **E**nvironmental concerns, **D**urability, **S**afety, **C**ost (economics), **A**esthetics, **M**aterials and **P**roduction. If you use this as a memory aid, you should be able to answer any question that asks about design factors. There are obviously additional areas contained within these headings, but it is a great help to have one word that reminds you of all the areas. For the rest of the questions in this section, you should think back through your course and the work you did in the Design Unit. This should help you answer the questions about the design process, sketching, modelling, specifications and the product evaluation activities you were involved with.

Section 2

Section 2 is worth 20 marks. It contains four to five questions. The first question in Section 2 will focus on the identification and justification of materials and processes related to the component parts of an existing commercially manufactured product. The remaining questions in this section will cover a range of commercial manufacturing topics contained within the Course Assessment Specification. These could range from the benefits or drawbacks of CAM through to other commercial manufacturing processes not covered in the first question within this section. Further information regarding the Course Assessment Specification for N5 Design and Manufacture is available via www.sqa.org.uk

Where marks are commonly lost

One of the major problems that markers find is the lack of description in students' answers. When asked about design factors in relation to a given product, such as a kettle, the usual response is:

"The kettle should be safe and durable."

Although this is correct, we could be talking about any product on the planet, for example a watch should also be safe and durable.

To gain full marks, you should make clear reference to the product being asked about, so if we answer again about the kettle, the answer should be:

"It needs to be safe because the body of the kettle could get very hot with the boiling water and you could burn yourself. It needs to be durable because during the lifespan of a kettle it may get banged in the kitchen sink when being filled and it should withstand these collisions."

When you look at the response above you can clearly see that we are talking about a kettle now and not a watch. Try to do this through the whole of the paper, specifically in Section 2 when each question is about a different product.

Another area where candidates answer poorly is within the product evaluation question. You should try to extend your answers to fully describe the activities you would carry out with reference to the product being asked about. Too often responses are simplistic, for example, when being asked about evaluating the ease of use of a vacuum cleaner:

"They should do a user trial."

Or when being asked about value for money of a vacuum cleaner:

"They should do a comparison with other products."

Once again, these answers are correct, but do not explain the activity in any detail and would therefore not attract full marks.

An exemplar answer would be:

"They should carry out a user trial, where a range of users vacuum an area of carpet and then describe how easy or difficult they found the vacuum cleaner to manoeuvre around small items of furniture.

They should look at a range of existing vacuum cleaners that perform similar functions and see what their selling price is. They could then compare the selling price to theirs and this will show if their vacuum cleaner is good value for money."

Where improvements could be made to achieve better grades

If you want to achieve a better grade you should think about the way you answer other questions, such as questions that ask for "properties of materials that make them suitable for a particular product".

If you try to explain the properties of HDPE it may be difficult and the ones you choose may not relate directly to the product being asked about. Try to list the properties the product needs to have to be successful at its function. If we take the example of a milk container made from HDPE, we can then say that HDPE can be recycled, it is available in a range of colours and it is non-toxic. These are all "things" that the milk container does because it is a milk container not because it is made of HDPE. All of your properties of materials questions can be answered this way if you refer to "what the product needs to do" rather than the material.

The ergonomics question is where you could rack up vital extra marks. This question can be answered in lots of ways, but it is a good idea to have a plan before you go into the exam in case the ergonomics question is in the paper.

Think about the three aspects of ergonomics: anthropometrics, physiology and psychology.

Try to write two answers for each area relating to the product in the question.

There is a simple formula to help you get full marks in this question.

For anthropometrics, pick a part of the product and then pick a part of the human body that should fit on/into that part. Link them together in a sentence and you get one mark. Do that twice to get full marks. E.g. Kettle: the handle of the kettle should fit the adult male palm width.

For physiology, pick a part of the product and then come up with a verb that you would do with that part. Link them together in a sentence and you get one mark. Do that twice to get full marks. E.g. Kettle: filling should be easy so the lid should be easy to open.

For psychology, pick a part of the product and then come up with a feeling or emotion to do with that part. Link them together in a sentence and you get one mark. Do that twice to get full marks. E.g. Kettle: the switch on the kettle should make a clicking sound to let you know that it is on.

Good luck!

Remember that the rewards for passing National 5 Design and Manufacture are well worth it! Your pass will help you get the future you want for yourself. In the exam, be confident in your own ability. If you're not sure how to answer a question trust your instincts and just give it a go anyway. Keep calm and don't panic! GOOD LUCK!

Study Skills – what you need to know to pass exams!

General exam revision: 20 top tips

When preparing for exams, it is easy to feel unsure of where to start or how to revise. This guide to general exam revision provides a good starting place, and, as these are very general tips, they can be applied to all your exams.

1. Start revising in good time.
Don't leave revision until the last minute – this will make you panic and it will be difficult to learn. Make a revision timetable that counts down the weeks to go.

2. Work to a study plan.
Set up sessions of work spread through the weeks ahead. Make sure each session has a focus and a clear purpose. What will you study, when and why? Be realistic about what you can achieve in each session, and don't be afraid to adjust your plans as needed.

3. Make sure you know exactly when your exams are.
Get your exam dates from the SQA website and use the timetable builder tool to create your own exam schedule. You will also get a personalised timetable from your school, but this might not be until close to the exam period.

4. Make sure that you know the topics that make up each course.
Studying is easier if material is in manageable chunks – why not use the SQA topic headings or create your own from your class notes? Ask your teacher for help on this if you are not sure.

5. Break the chunks up into even smaller bits.
The small chunks should be easier to cope with. Remember that they fit together to make larger ideas. Even the process of chunking down will help!

6. Ask yourself these key questions for each course:
- Are all topics compulsory or are there choices?
- Which topics seem to come up time and time again?
- Which topics are your strongest and which are your weakest?

Use your answers to these questions to work out how much time you will need to spend revising each topic.

7. Make sure you know what to expect in the exam.
The subject-specific introduction to this book will help with this. Make sure you can answer these questions:
- How is the paper structured?
- How much time is there for each part of the exam?
- What types of question are involved? These will vary depending on the subject so read the subject-specific section carefully.

8. Past papers are a vital revision tool!
Use past papers to support your revision wherever possible. This book contains the answers and mark schemes too – refer to these carefully when checking your work. Using the mark scheme is useful; even if you don't manage to get all the marks available first time when you first practise, it helps you identify how to extend and develop your answers to get more marks next time – and of course, in the real exam.

9. Use study methods that work well for you.
People study and learn in different ways. Reading and looking at diagrams suits some students. Others prefer to listen and hear material – what about reading out loud or getting a friend or family member to do this for you? You could also record and play back material.

10. There are three tried and tested ways to make material stick in your long-term memory:
- Practising – e.g. rehearsal, repeating
- Organising – e.g. making drawings, lists, diagrams, tables, memory aids
- Elaborating – e.g. incorporating the material into a story or an imagined journey

11. Learn actively.
Most people prefer to learn actively – for example, making notes, highlighting, redrawing and redrafting, making up memory aids, or writing past paper answers. A good way to stay engaged and inspired is to mix and match these methods – find the combination that best suits you. This is likely to vary depending on the topic or subject.

12. Be an expert.

Be sure to have a few areas in which you feel you are an expert. This often works because at least some of them will come up, which can boost confidence.

13. Try some visual methods.

Use symbols, diagrams, charts, flashcards, post-it notes etc. Don't forget – the brain takes in chunked images more easily than loads of text.

14. Remember – practice makes perfect.

Work on difficult areas again and again. Look and read – then test yourself. You cannot do this too much.

15. Try past papers against the clock.

Practise writing answers in a set time. This is a good habit from the start but is especially important when you get closer to exam time.

16. Collaborate with friends.

Test each other and talk about the material – this can really help. Two brains are better than one! It is amazing how talking about a problem can help you solve it.

17. Know your weaknesses.

Ask your teacher for help to identify what you don't know. Try to do this as early as possible. If you are having trouble, it is probably with a difficult topic, so your teacher will already be aware of this – most students will find it tough.

18. Have your materials organised and ready.

Know what is needed for each exam:
- Do you need a calculator or a ruler?
- Should you have pencils as well as pens?
- Will you need water or paper tissues?

19. Make full use of school resources.

Find out what support is on offer:
- Are there study classes available?
- When is the library open?
- When is the best time to ask for extra help?
- Can you borrow textbooks, study guides, past papers, etc.?
- Is school open for Easter revision?

20. Keep fit and healthy!

Try to stick to a routine as much as possible, including with sleep. If you are tired, sluggish or dehydrated, it is difficult to see how concentration is even possible. Combine study with relaxation, drink plenty of water, eat sensibly, and get fresh air and exercise – all these things will help more than you could imagine. Good luck!

NATIONAL 5
2017

FOR OFFICIAL USE

N5

National Qualifications 2017

Mark

X719/75/01

Design and Manufacture

TUESDAY, 2 MAY
1:00 PM — 2:30 PM

Fill in these boxes and read what is printed below.

Full name of centre

Town

Forename(s)

Surname

Number of seat

Date of birth
Day Month Year

Scottish candidate number

Total marks — 60

SECTION 1 — 24 marks

Attempt ALL questions.

SECTION 2 — 36 marks

Attempt ALL questions.

Write your answers clearly in the spaces provided in this booklet. Additional space for answers is provided at the end of this booklet. If you use this space you must clearly identify the question number you are attempting.

Use **blue** or **black** ink.

Before leaving the examination room you must give this booklet to the Invigilator; if you do not, you may lose all the marks for this paper.

SQA

SECTION 1 — 24 MARKS
Attempt ALL questions

1. A DVD holder is shown below.

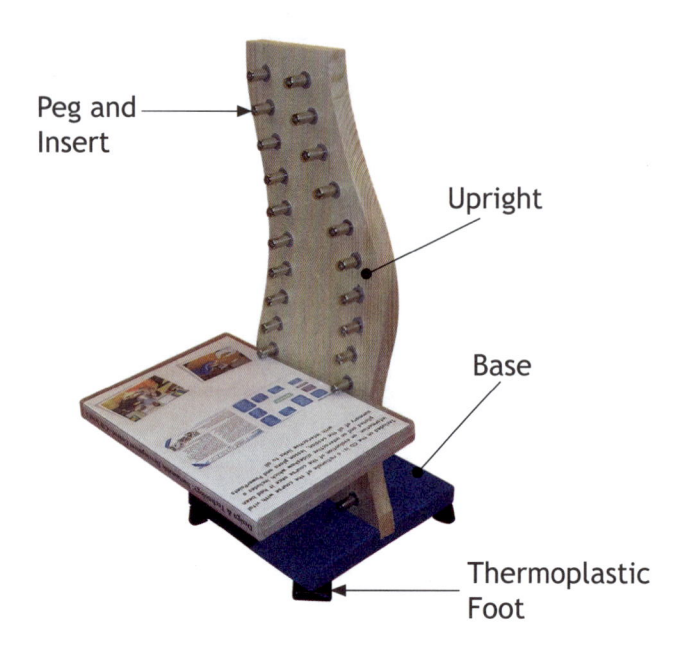

   (a) The pegs and inserts used are bought as "standard components".

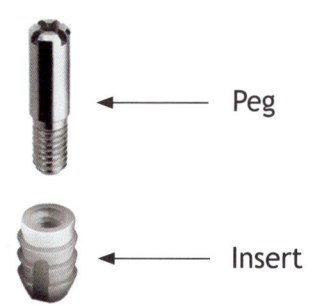

   (i) Explain what is meant by the term "*standard components*".   1

   (ii) State **two** benefits of using standard components.   2

Page two

1. (continued)

    (b) The board for the upright and base was made by gluing strips of wood, edge to edge as shown in the picture below.

    — Board

    (i) Describe **one** benefit of cramping the wood for the upright and base in this way. 1

    _____

    _____

    _____

    (ii) Describe **two** environmental considerations when selecting the type of wood for a product. 2

    _____

    _____

    _____

    _____

    _____

    _____

    _____

[Turn over

1. (continued)

    (c) A model of the DVD holder was tested as shown below.

    (i) Describe the information that could be gained from testing the model. **2**

    _____

    _____

    _____

    _____

    The model was mainly made from MDF.

    (ii) State **one** reason why this material is suitable for this type of model. **1**

    _____

    _____

    (d) A template was used to mark out the shape of the upright. State **two** advantages of using a template. **2**

    _____

    _____

    _____

    _____

1. (continued)

   (e) The marked out shape of the upright is shown below.

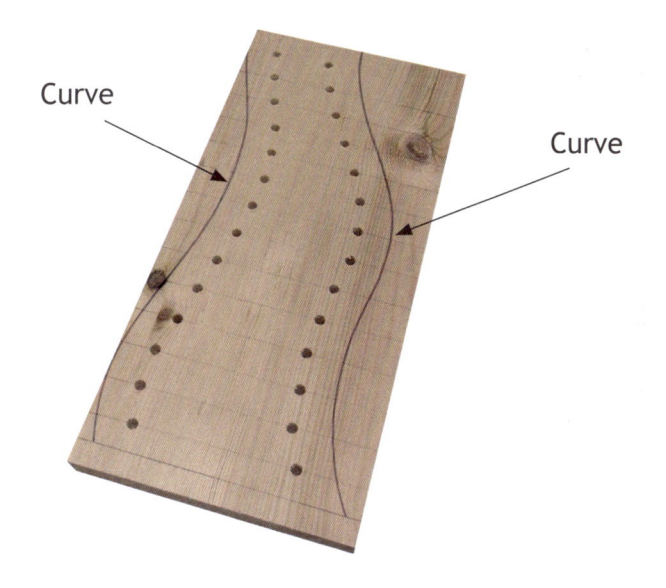

   Curve   Curve

   (i) With reference to workshop tools and processes, describe **two** stages in cutting and shaping the curves. 2

   _____
   _____
   _____
   _____
   _____
   _____
   _____

   [Turn over

1. (e) (continued)

   (ii) The housing joint used to join the upright to the base is shown below.

   With reference to workshop tools and processes, describe **four** stages required to mark out and manufacture this type of joint.

   (*You must refer to marking out and manufacturing to gain full marks.*)   4

1. (e) (continued)

The upright was finished with clear varnish.

(iii) With reference to workshop tools **and** processes, describe **two** stages in the preparation of the wood before applying the finish. **2**

(iv) State **one** benefit of using clear varnish as a finish for the upright. **1**

[Turn over

1. (continued)

   (f) The thermoplastic foot was manufactured from the marked out blank as shown below.

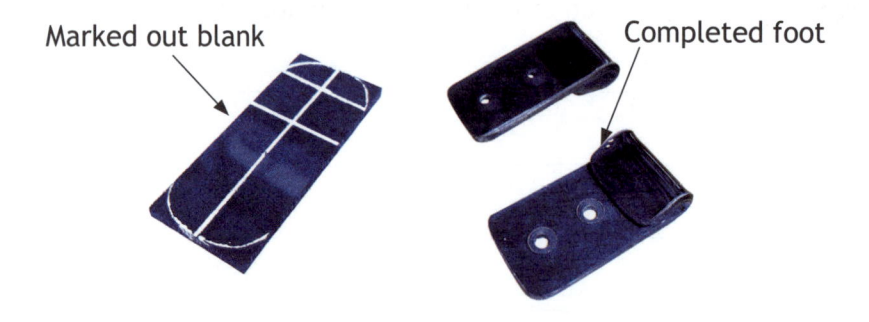

   Marked out blank

   Completed foot

   With reference to workshop tools and processes, describe **four** stages in the manufacture of the thermoplastic foot, **after it has been marked out**. 4

[Turn over for next question

DO NOT WRITE ON THIS PAGE

SECTION 2 — 36 MARKS

Attempt ALL questions

2. Designers consider aesthetics and ergonomics in the design of products such as the pram shown below.

   (a) Describe **four** aesthetics aspects of the pram. 4

2. (continued)

   (b) Describe how ergonomics has influenced the design of the pram. 6

3. The storage unit shown below is sold as a "flat pack" product.

    (a) Describe **one** benefit to the consumer of *"flat pack"* products. 1

3. (continued)

(b) The manufacturer used CNC and CADCAM technologies during the manufacture of the storage unit.

Describe **two** benefits to the manufacturer of using these technologies. **2**

(c) Designers generate new ideas to meet the needs of consumers.

Describe how **one** idea generation technique would be carried out.

(Sketches may be used to illustrate your answer in the box below.) **2**

[Turn over

4. An inkjet printer is shown below.

ABS outer casing

(a) The printer was mass produced. All mass production processes have initial set up costs.

(i) State **two** of the initial set up costs. 2

(ii) State **one** suitable manufacturing process for the outer casing **and** justify your answer. 2

(iii) Describe **two** reasons why ABS is a suitable material for the manufacture of the outer casing. 2

4. (a) (continued)

   (iv) The outer casing is manufactured from ABS.

   State the name of one other suitable thermoplastic that could have been used for the outer casing. **1**

   _____

   _____

(b) The symbols shown below are commonly found on electrical products.

   State **one** purpose of these types of symbol. **1**

   _____

   _____

[Turn over

5. A pair of running shoes is shown below.

    (a) The manufacturer wants to carry out an evaluation of the running shoes.

    Describe how the following aspects of the running shoes could be evaluated.

    (Note: *a different evaluation technique must be used for each aspect*.)

    (i) Function. — 2

    (ii) Value for money. — 2

5. (continued)

(b) There is a wide variety of running shoes available to consumers. Designers need to find ways of marketing their running shoes in order to make them stand out from the competition.

Describe **two** marketing techniques that a design team may use to promote their running shoes.   **2**

_____

_____

_____

_____

(c) A range of graphic techniques was used during the development of the running shoes.

State **two** types of graphic technique that could have been used during the development of the running shoes.   **2**

_____

_____

(d) During the development of the running shoes a model of the sole was rapid prototyped using a 3D printer.

Describe **two** benefits to the manufacturer of rapid prototyping.   **2**

_____

_____

_____

_____

_____

[Turn over for next question

5. (continued)

(e) Manufacturers often choose to mass produce their products in developing countries.

(i) Describe **one** benefit to manufacturers of choosing to operate in developing countries. **1**

(ii) Describe **two** "*social expectations*" that consumers would have of a manufacturer operating in a developing country. **2**

[END OF QUESTION PAPER]

ADDITIONAL SPACE FOR ANSWERS

ADDITIONAL SPACE FOR ANSWERS

NATIONAL 5
2017 Specimen Question Paper

FOR OFFICIAL USE

N5

National Qualifications SPECIMEN ONLY

S819/75/01

Mark

Design and Manufacture

Date — Not applicable

Duration — 1 hour 45 minutes

Fill in these boxes and read what is printed below.

Full name of centre

Town

Forename(s)

Surname

Number of seat

Date of birth

Day   Month   Year   Scottish candidate number

Total marks — 80

SECTION 1 — 60 marks

Attempt ALL questions.

SECTION 2 — 20 marks

Attempt ALL questions.

Write your answers clearly in the spaces provided in this booklet. Additional space for answers is provided at the end of this booklet. If you use this space you must clearly identify the question number you are attempting.

Show all working and units where appropriate.

Use **blue** or **black** ink.

Before leaving the examination room you must give your answer booklet to the Invigilator; if you do not, you may lose all the marks for this paper.

SQA

SECTION 1 — 60 marks

Attempt ALL questions

1. A design proposal for a table lamp is shown below.

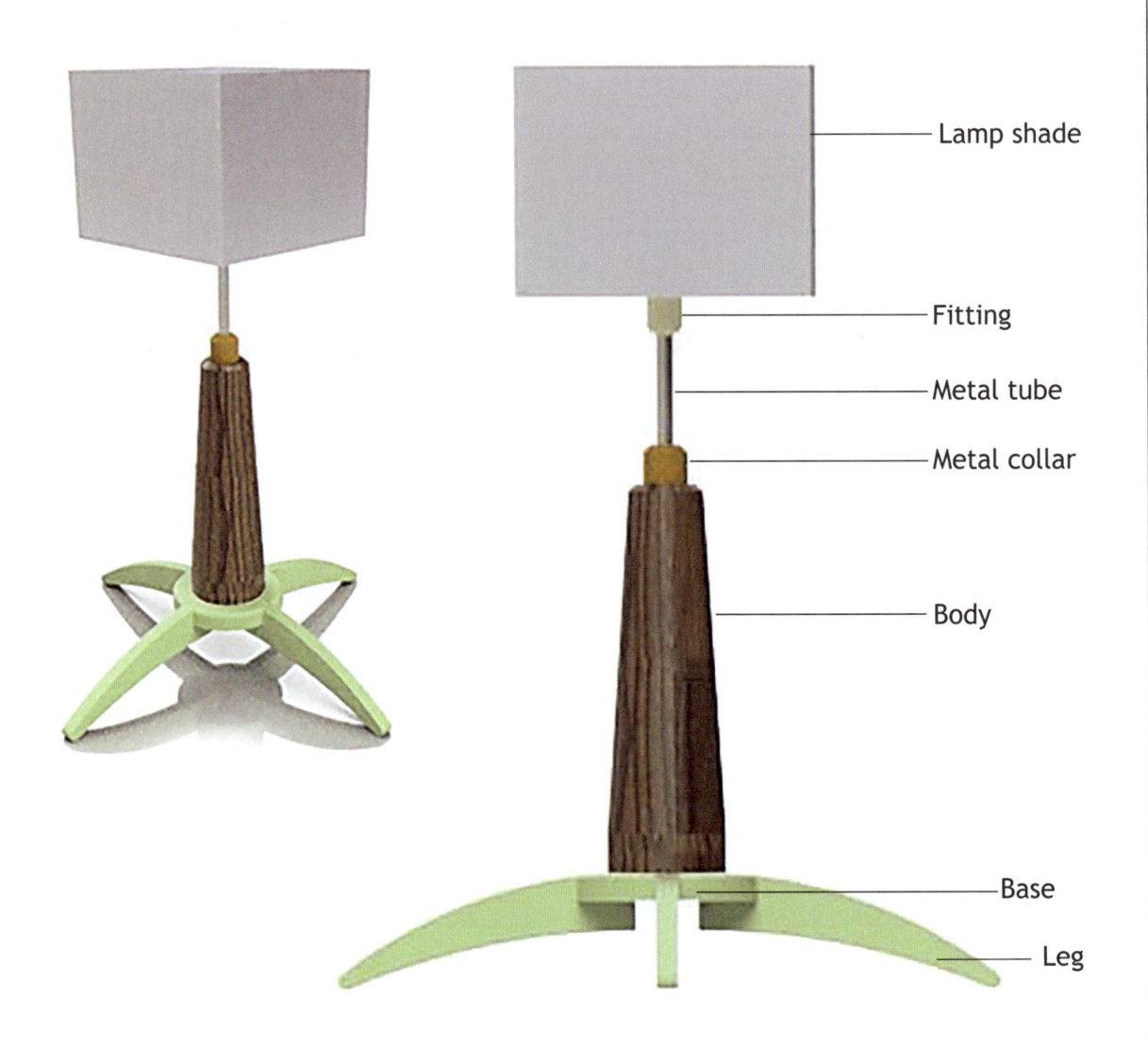

   (a) The lamp is made from different materials.

   (i) Name a suitable dark coloured hardwood for the body of the lamp. 1

   _____

   (ii) Name a suitable yellow-coloured alloy for the metal collar. 1

   _____

1. (continued)

   (b) The body of the lamp will be manufactured on a wood turning lathe.

   Outline **two** safety checks that must be carried out on the wood turning lathe before the body is manufactured.

   2

   _____

   _____

   _____

   _____

   [Turn over

1. (continued)

    (c) A wood turning blank is required for the body of the lamp.

    (i) Describe how to mark out **and** remove the corners of the blank in preparation for turning. You must refer to workshop tools in your answer.

    (Sketches may be used to illustrate your answer.) 4

1. (c) (continued)

A shoulder has been turned accurately to the sizes shown on the drawing. The shoulder will join the body to the base.

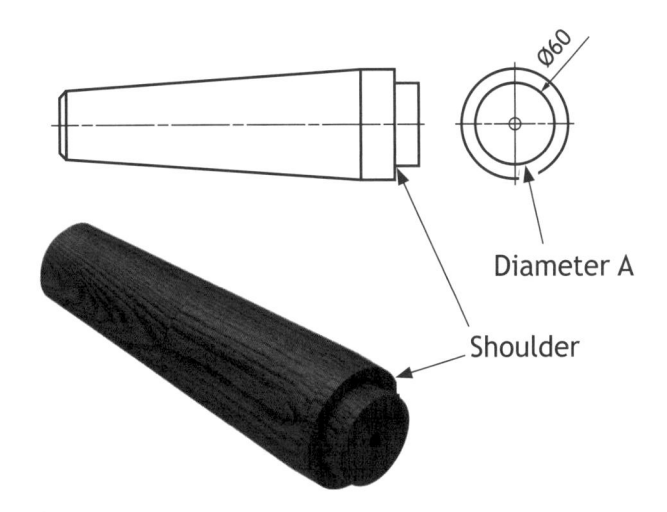

(ii) Name the lathe tool that should be used to create the shoulder. **1**

_____

(iii) Name a hand tool that could be used to check diameter A is 60 mm. **1**

_____

[Turn over

1. (continued)

    (d) The part of the base shown below was cut and shaped from MDF.

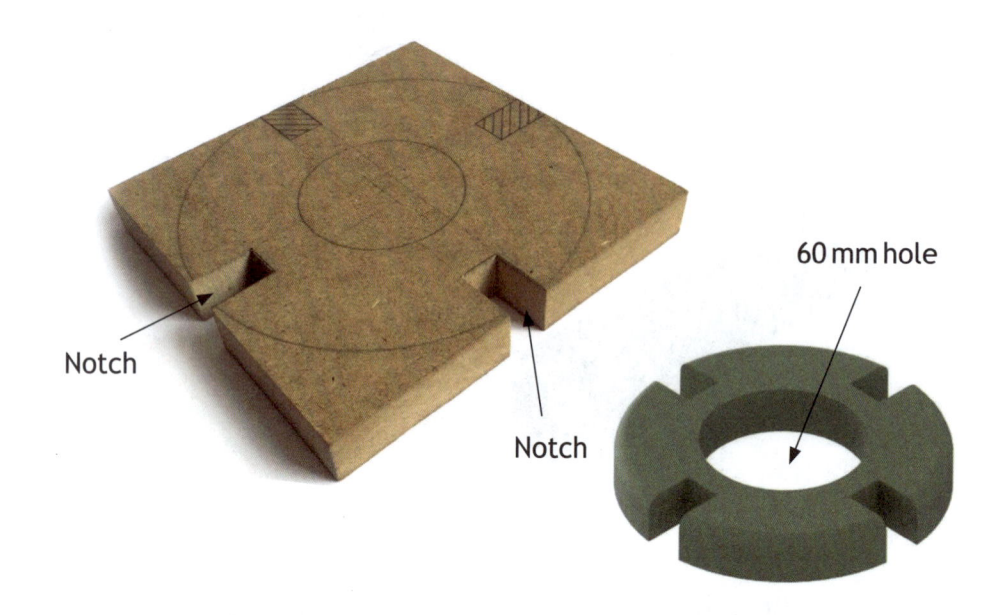

    Notch

    Notch

    60 mm hole

    (i) Describe how the notches to join the legs could be cut out accurately, with reference to workshop tools.

    (*Sketches may be used to illustrate your answer.*) **2**

1. (d) (continued)

    (ii) Name the drill bit that could be used to drill the 60 mm hole.   1

  (e) A template was used to mark out the four MDF legs of the base.

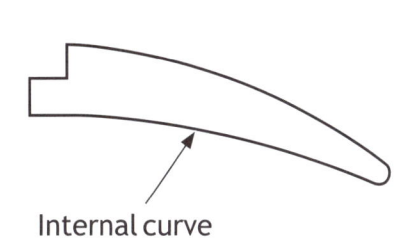

Internal curve

    (i) Explain **two** reasons for using a template to mark out the legs.   2

    (ii) Name the hand tool that would be used to cut the internal curve.   1

[Turn over

1. (continued)

   (f) The metal to make the collar was cut to length then turned on a centre lathe.

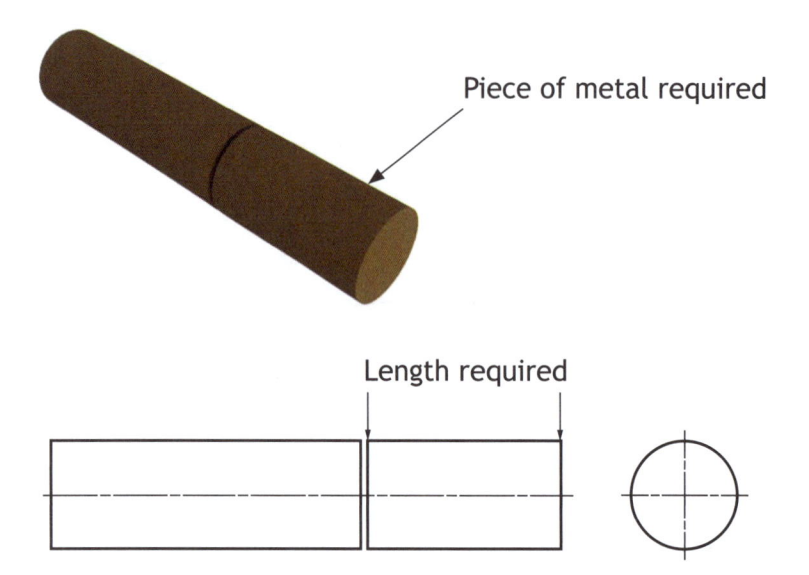

   (i) Name the vice that should be used to hold the metal while it is being cut. **1**

   (ii) Name a hand tool that could be used to cut the metal to length. **1**

   Before the metal collar was drilled, a number of processes were carried out on the centre lathe.

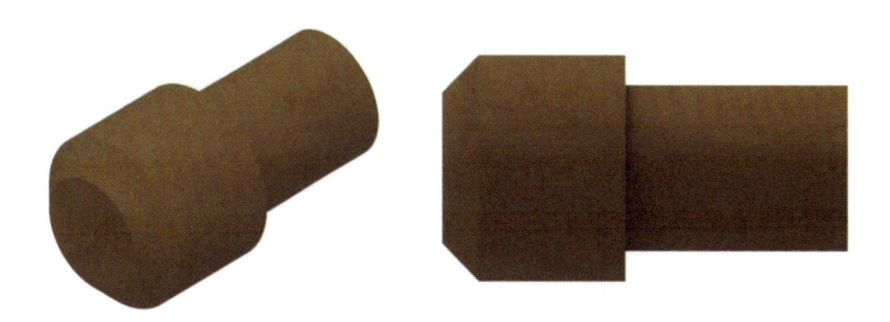

1. (f) (continued)

    (iii) Name **three** processes that would be carried out on a centre lathe to manufacture the metal collar.   3

    _____

    _____

    _____

   (g) A hole was drilled to allow an internal thread to be cut.

    (i) Explain why a centre drill has to be used before the hole can be drilled.   1

    _____

    _____

    _____

[Turn over

1. (g) (continued)

An external thread was cut at both ends of the metal tube. This allows the light fitting to attach to the collar of the lamp.

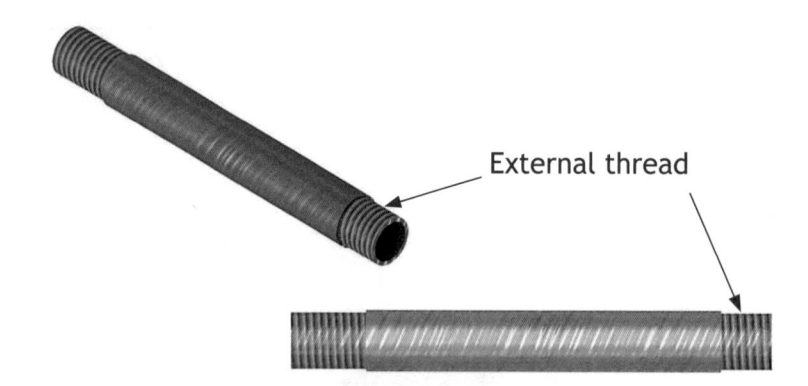

External thread

(ii) Name the hand tool that would be used to cut the external thread. **1**

(iii) It is important that a good quality thread is cut. Describe how this can be done. **2**

1. (continued)

   (h) Sketches were produced to help plan the tasks required to manufacture the lamp shade.

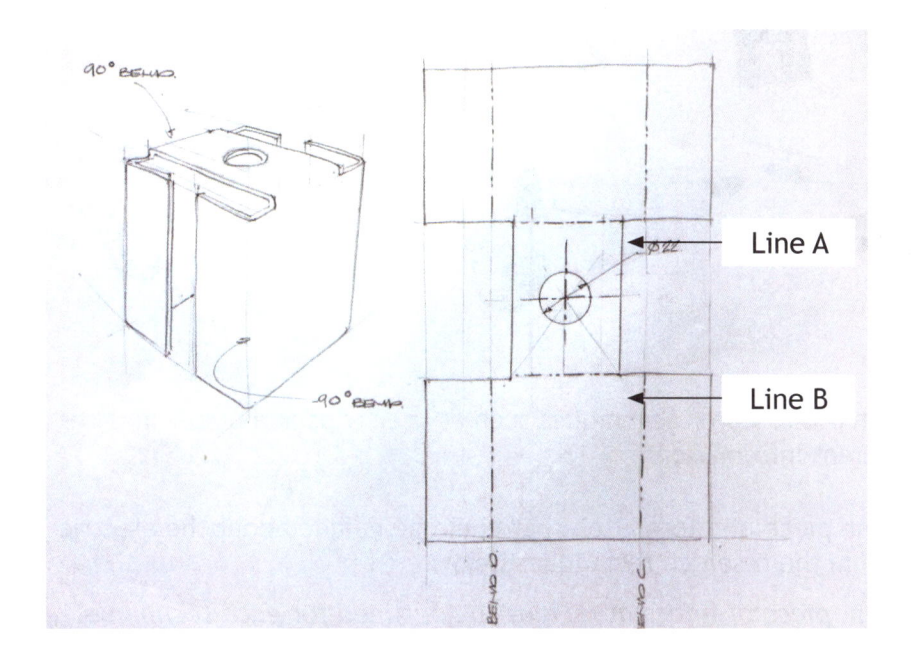

   The lamp shade is manufactured from acrylic.

   (i) State **two** reasons why acrylic is a suitable choice for the lamp shade. **2**

   _____

   _____

   (ii) The acrylic has to be heated before forming the 90 degree bends. State the name of the equipment that should be used to heat the acrylic along lines A and B. **1**

   _____

   (iii) The edges of the acrylic were finished before the lamp shade was formed. Explain why the edges of the acrylic should be finished before it is formed into shape. **2**

   _____

   _____

   _____

   _____

   [Turn over

2. Designers used research to improve the design of the electric scooter shown below.

Designers often use research techniques such as user trips and questionnaires to gather different information:

(a) Outline **one** piece of information that could be gained about the electric scooter from the research techniques below.

(*A different piece of information must be outlined for each technique.*)

(i) a user trip 1

_____

(ii) a questionnaire 1

_____

2. (continued)

   (b) Select **one** of these research techniques from the options below. Tick the box (✓).

   ☐ User trip

   ☐ Research questionnaire

   Describe key stages for the research technique you have selected. **3**

   Designers often use a specification when developing a design proposal.

   (c) Describe how a specification could be used during the exploration and refinement stages of the design process. **2**

   Exploration:

   Refinement:

[Turn over

Page thirteen

3. A page of initial ideas for a clock design is shown below.

The designer could have used morphological analysis or brainstorming to generate a range of ideas.

Select **one** of the idea generation techniques from the options below. Tick the box (✓).

☐ Morphological analysis

☐ Brainstorming

Describe the key stages of **one** of these idea generation techniques.

3

_____

_____

_____

_____

_____

_____

4. Sketches and drawings are used at different stages of the design process.

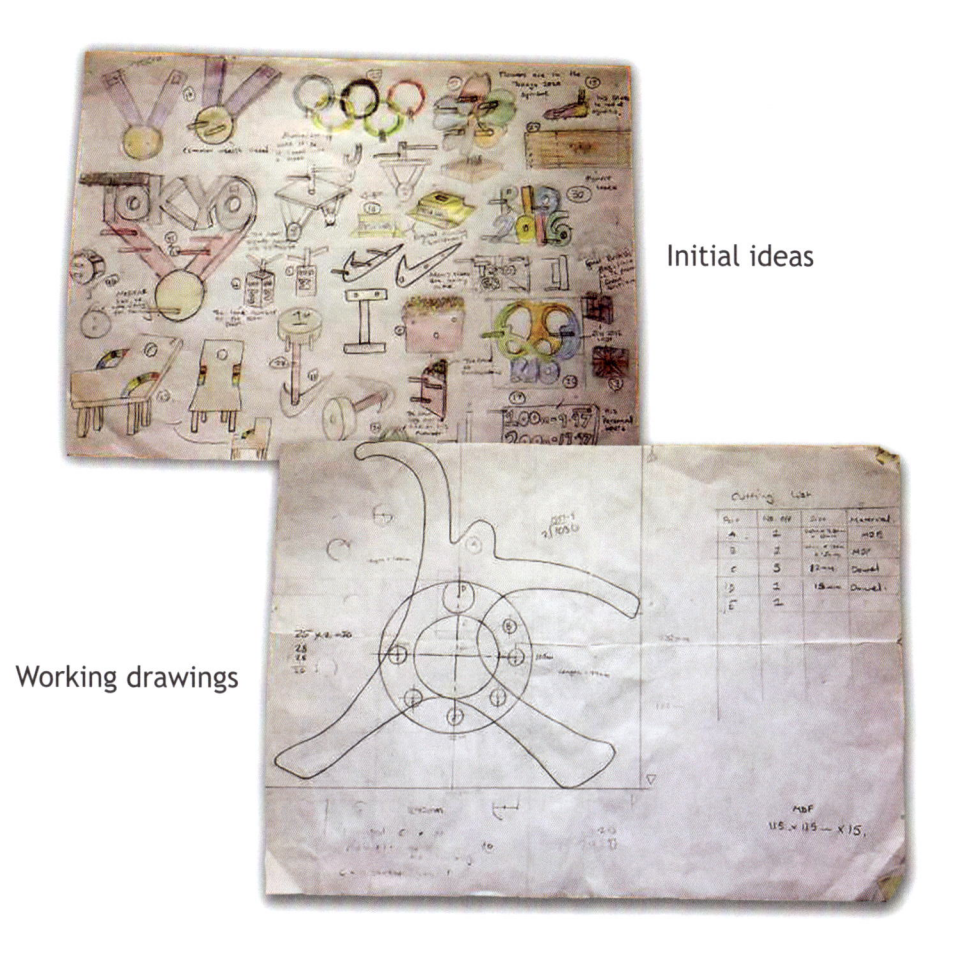

Initial ideas

Working drawings

(a) Explain why sketching is a suitable technique to use when generating ideas.

2

[Turn over

4. (continued)

   (b) Describe the reasons for producing working drawings. **2**

5. Different types of models can be used throughout the design process.

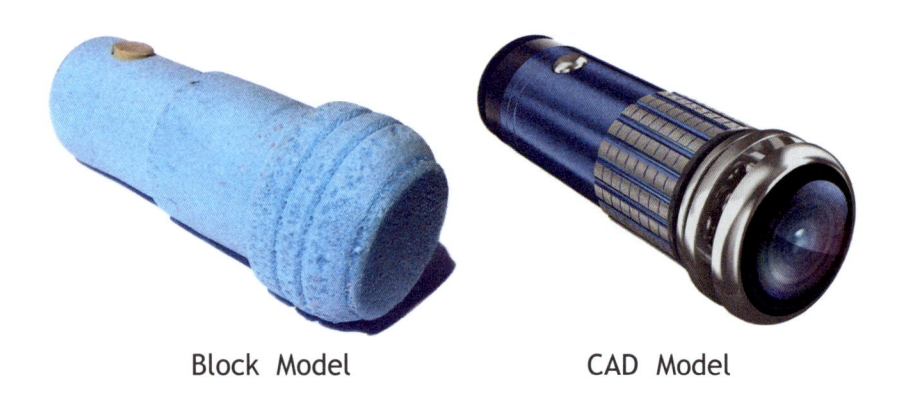

   Block Model   CAD Model

   (a) Outline **two** reasons for using block models during the design process. **2**

   (b) Outline **two** reasons for using CAD models when presenting ideas to the client. **2**

6. Designers will have considered a range of design factors when designing the child's trike below.

   (a) Describe how the use of anthropometrics data has influenced the sizes of the trike. You should refer to specific data and parts of the trike in your answer. **4**

[Turn over

6. (continued)

   (b) To be a commercial success the trike has to appeal to both children and parents.

   (i) Outline **two** reasons why the aesthetics of the trike would appeal to children. 2

   (ii) Outline **two** reasons other than aesthetics that would make the trike appealing to parents. 2

7. (a) Technology push has led to an increased number of gadgets to control the modern home.

Describe what is meant by technology push. **2**

(b) Describe the benefits of launching a new product under a successful brand name. **2**

[Turn over

SECTION 2 — 20 marks
Attempt ALL questions

8. The pencil case and its contents shown below have been mass produced using a range of materials and processes.

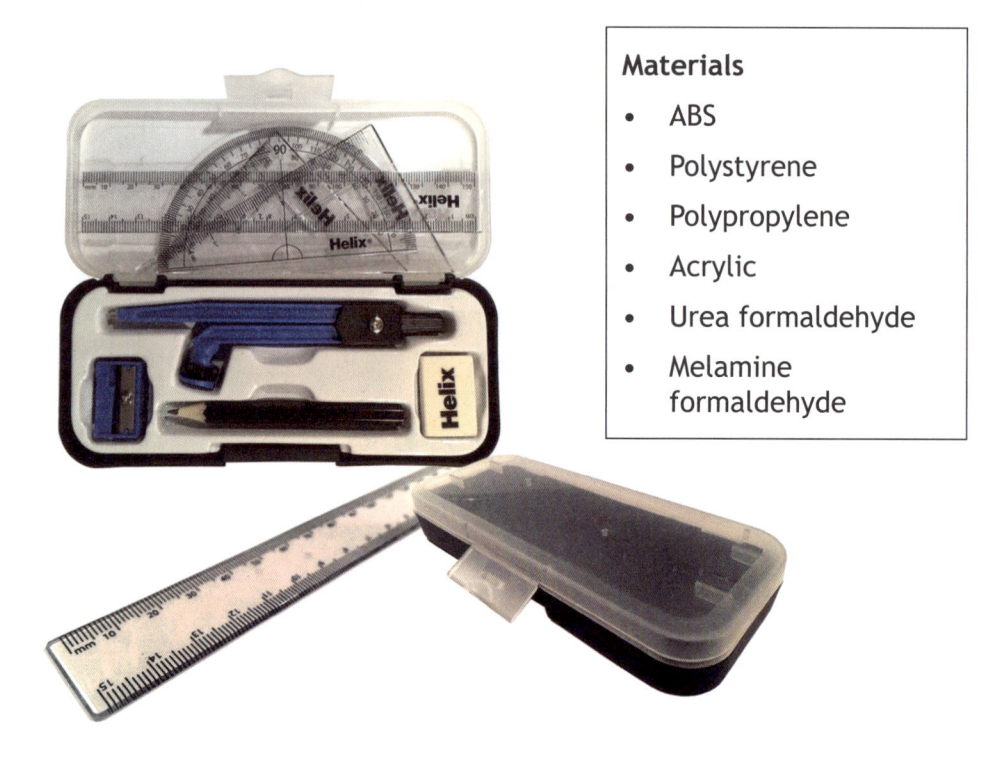

Materials
- ABS
- Polystyrene
- Polypropylene
- Acrylic
- Urea formaldehyde
- Melamine formaldehyde

(a) Select a material from the list provided and explain why it would be suitable for the items below.

(A different material must be selected for each item.)

(i) Ruler

(ii) Case lid

8. (continued)

The case insert was manufactured by vacuum forming.

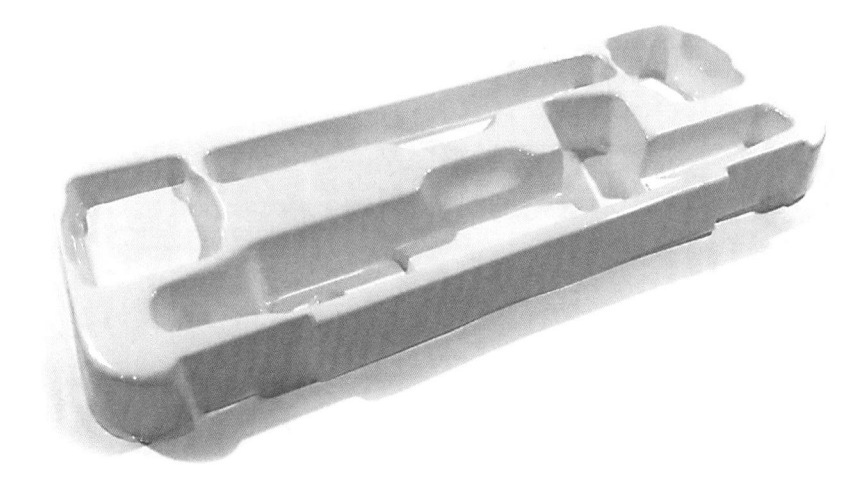

(b) The pattern contains the following features. State a manufacturing reason for each.

(i) Rounded edges 1

(ii) Vent holes 1

(iii) Tapered sides 1

[Turn over

8. **(continued)**

The set of compasses shown below has been mass produced using different materials and processes.

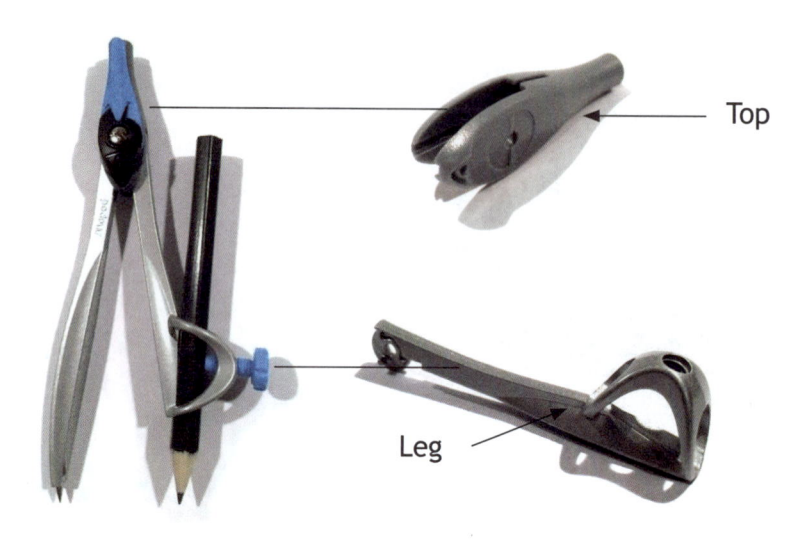

The top of the set of compasses was created by injection moulding.

(c) State **two** identifying features that would show this. 2

_____

_____

The legs of the set of compasses are made from a metal alloy.

(d) Name a suitable mass production process to manufacture the legs. 1

_____

9. Computer aided manufacture (CAM) is widely used in mass production.

Explain **two** reasons for using CAM to mass produce products.

[Turn over

10. Many furniture companies design their furniture incorporating standard components such as knock-down fittings.

Describe the benefits to the consumer **and** the manufacturer of using knock-down fittings.

3

11. Manufacturing technologies are widely used by companies to mass produce affordable products. These technologies can impact on the environment and the workforce.

(a) Describe **one** benefit and **one** drawback that manufacturing technologies have had on the workforce.

Benefit:

_____

_____

Drawback:

_____

_____

[Turn over

11. (continued)

(b) Describe **three** ways that manufacturing technologies impact on the environment. 3

[END OF SPECIMEN QUESTION PAPER]

ADDITIONAL SPACE FOR ANSWERS

ADDITIONAL SPACE FOR ANSWERS

NATIONAL 5

2018

FOR OFFICIAL USE

N5

National Qualifications 2018

Mark

X819/75/01

Design and Manufacture

FRIDAY, 18 MAY
1:00 PM — 2:45 PM

Fill in these boxes and read what is printed below.

Full name of centre

Town

Forename(s)

Surname

Number of seat

Date of birth
Day   Month   Year

Scottish candidate number

Total marks — 80

SECTION 1 — 60 marks

Attempt ALL questions.

SECTION 2 — 20 marks

Attempt ALL questions.

Write your answers clearly in the spaces provided in this booklet. Additional space for answers is provided at the end of this booklet. If you use this space you must clearly identify the question number you are attempting.

Use **blue** or **black** ink.

Before leaving the examination room you must give this booklet to the Invigilator; if you do not, you may lose all the marks for this paper.

SQA

SECTION 1 — 60 MARKS
Attempt ALL questions

1. A design proposal for a set of educational scales is shown below.

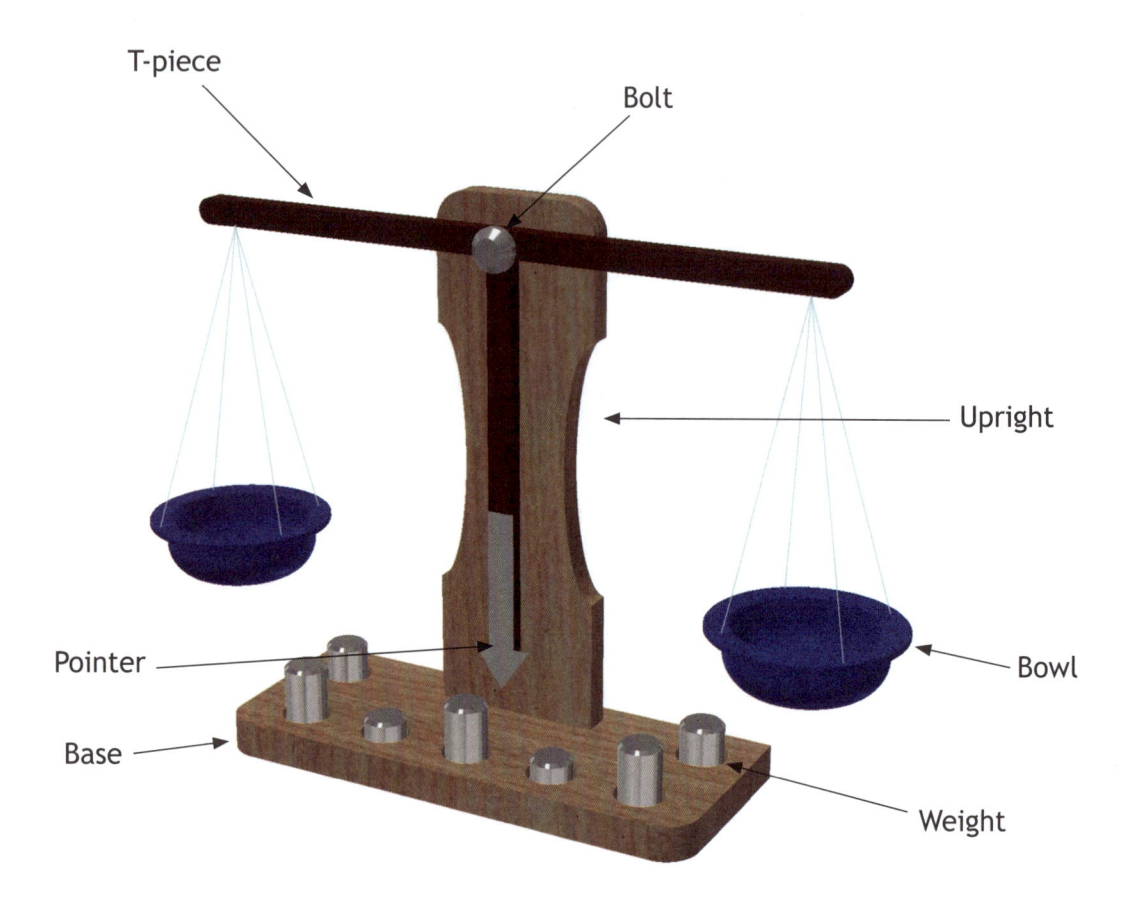

   Labels: T-piece, Bolt, Upright, Pointer, Base, Bowl, Weight

   (a) Red pine was used in the manufacture of the base and upright.

      (i) Name an alternative softwood that could be used.   1

   _____

1. (a) (continued)

   (ii) Two pieces of softwood were joined together to make the base.

   Describe how to join the pieces of softwood together. You must refer to workshop tools in your answer.

   (Sketches may be used to illustrate your answer in the box below.)   **2**

1. (continued)

(b) The finished base is shown below.

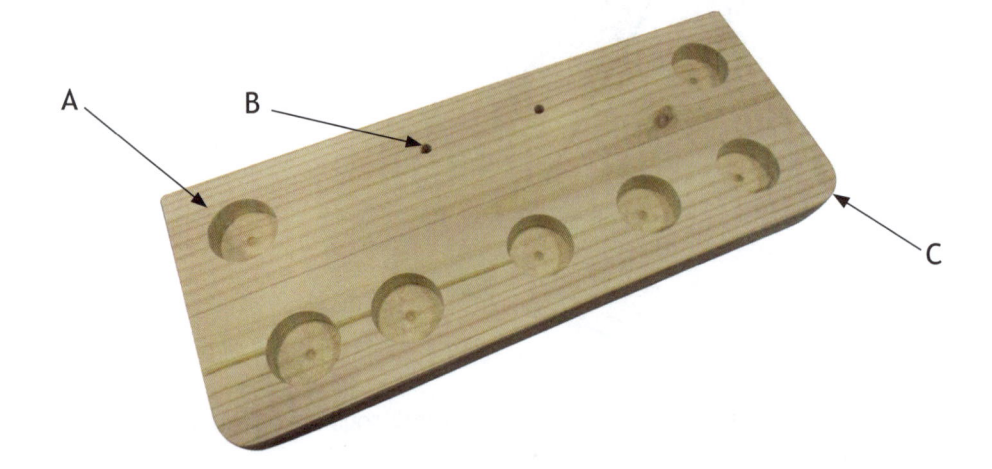

(i) Name the type of drill bit that should be used to create the flat-bottomed hole at A.

(ii) Name the type of drill bit that should be used to create the hole at B.

(iii) Name a machine that could be used to form the curve at C.

(iv) The holes on the underside of the base were countersunk.

State why the holes were countersunk.

1. (continued)

    (c) The upright is shown below.

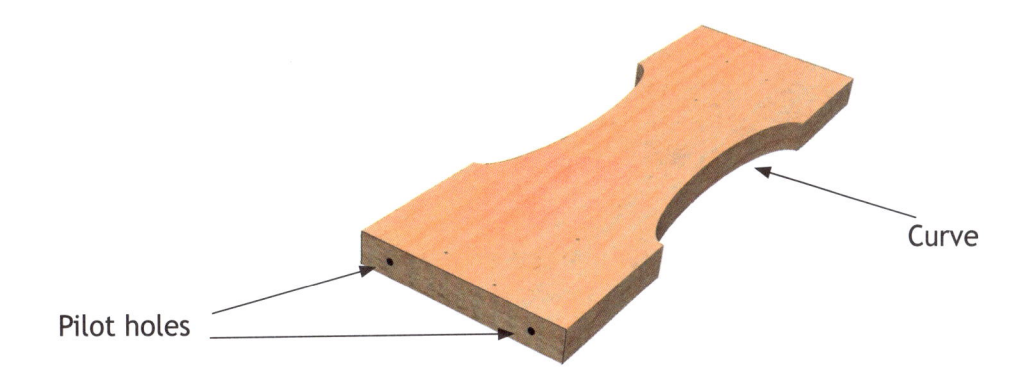

    Pilot holes were made and curves cut in the upright before it was screwed to the base.

    (i) Name the hand tool that should be used to create the pilot holes. **1**

    _____

    (ii) Name a hand tool that could be used to cut the curves. **1**

    _____

    The upright and base were finished with wax instead of varnish.

    (iii) Explain why wax would have been used instead of varnish. **2**

    _____

    _____

    _____

    _____

    _____

    _____

    _____

[Turn over

1. (continued)

    (d) A housing was used in the manufacture of the T-piece.

    Describe how the housing could be marked and cut out accurately. You must refer to workshop tools in your answer.

    (Sketches may be used to illustrate your answer in the box below.)   4

1. (continued)

   (e) The bolt and weight were created on a centre lathe.

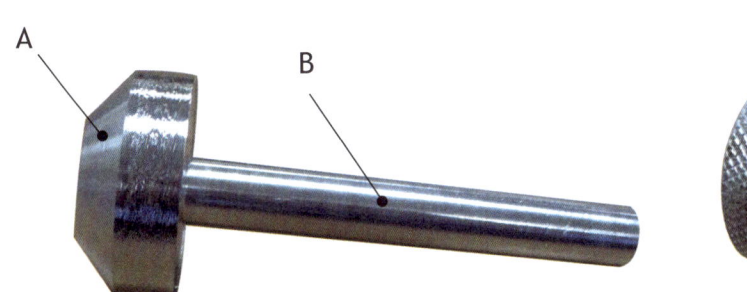

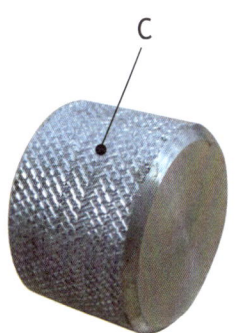

   (i) Name the processes that would be carried out on a centre lathe to create the features at A, B and C.

   A _____

   B _____

   C _____

   (ii) Having created features A and B, adjustments were made to the centre lathe to create feature C.

   State **two** adjustments that would need to be made to the centre lathe to create the textured feature on part C.

   _____

   _____

   _____

   _____

   [Turn over

1. **(continued)**

    (f) The bowls were made from a square piece of acrylic sheet using a former and then cut to shape.

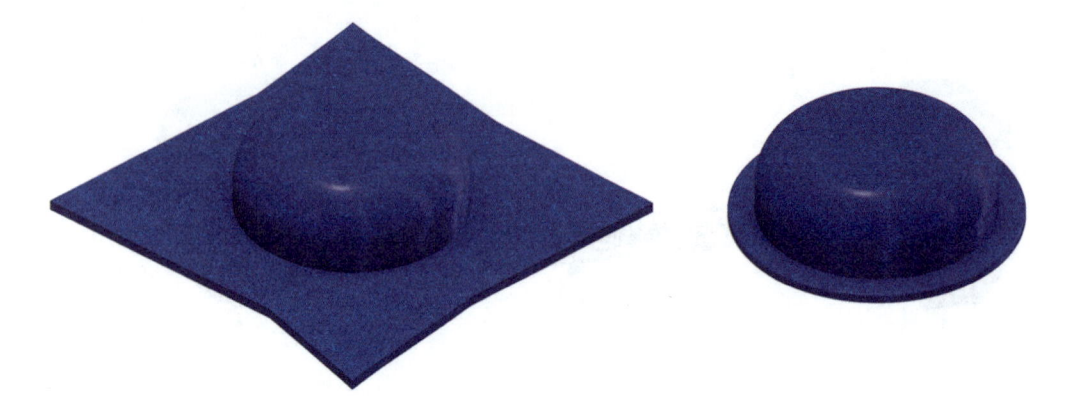

    (i) Explain why a former would be used to create the acrylic bowls. **2**

    _____
    _____
    _____
    _____
    _____

    (ii) Name the piece of equipment that would be used to heat the acrylic before it is formed. **1**

    _____

    (iii) Name a machine tool that could be used to cut out the circular shape. **1**

    _____

    (iv) Describe how the edge of the acrylic would be finished after sawing. **2**

    _____
    _____
    _____
    _____

1. (continued)

(g) The pointer was made from a piece of sheet metal.

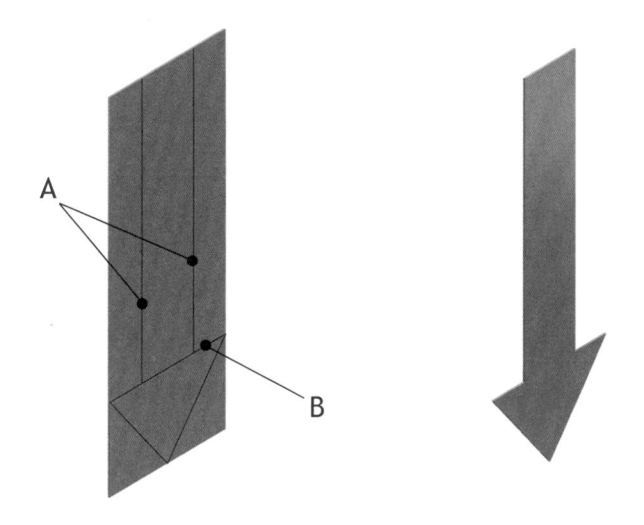

(i) Name a suitable silver-coloured, non-ferrous metal that could be used for the pointer. **1**

(ii) Name the tool that should be used to mark the two parallel lines at A. **1**

(iii) Name the tool that should be used with a scriber to mark the line B at a 90 degree angle to A. **1**

(iv) Name a hand tool that could be used to cut out the shape of the pointer. **1**

[Turn over

2. A variety of techniques can be used to gather information.

   (a) Explain the benefits of using a questionnaire to gather information. **3**

   (b) The information gathered from questionnaires can be used in the development of a specification.

   Describe how the specification can be used during the development of a design proposal. **2**

3. Morphological analysis is often used to generate ideas.

   (a) Describe the key stages of morphological analysis. **3**

3. (continued)

    (b) Name another idea generation technique. **1**

    _____

4. Computer generated graphics are often used during the development of products.

    Describe **three** benefits of using computer generated graphics during the development of products. **3**

    _____
    _____
    _____
    _____
    _____
    _____

    [Turn over

5. Modelling techniques were used during the design of the blender shown below.

Explain the reasons for using the following modelling techniques when developing the blender:

(*Different reasons must be given for each technique.*)

(a) A sketch model. 2

_____

_____

_____

_____

(b) A full-scale model. 2

_____

_____

_____

_____

6. The backpacks shown below were designed for two different target markets.

Backpack A

Backpack B

Hill walkers

Children

(a) Describe how the function and aesthetics of the backpacks have been influenced by their target markets.

(You may refer to one or both of the backpacks in your answer.)

(i) Function. **2**

(ii) Aesthetics. **2**

6. (continued)

(b) To ensure the backpacks were commercially successful the design team employed marketing techniques.

State **two** marketing techniques that could be used to improve sales. 2

_____

_____

7. A child's camera is shown below.

(a) Describe how ergonomics may have influenced the design of the child's camera. 4

_____

_____

_____

_____

_____

_____

_____

_____

7. (continued)

(b) Describe how performance may have influenced the design of the child's camera. **2**

(c) The design of products such as cameras has evolved over the years because of technology push.

Describe what is meant by technology push. **2**

[Turn over

SECTION 2 — 20 MARKS

Attempt ALL questions

8. The handle of a craft knife and its packaging have been mass produced using different materials and processes.

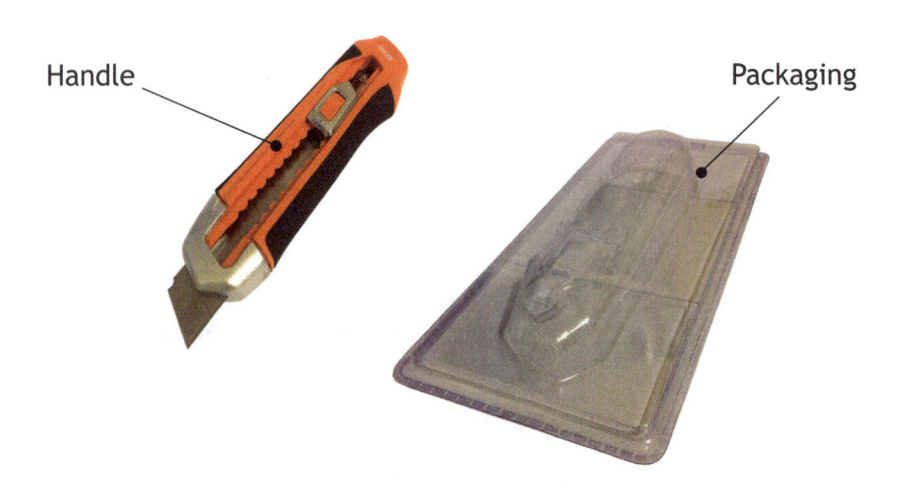

Handle

Packaging

(a) Identify a thermoplastic which could have been used in the production of each of the items below and explain why it would be suitable.

   (*A different thermoplastic and explanation must be given for each item.*)

   (i) Handle.

   Thermoplastic: _____

   Suitable because _____

   _____

   _____

   (ii) Packaging.

   Thermoplastic: _____

   Suitable because _____

   _____

   _____

   _____

Page sixteen

8. (continued)

   (b) Name the process that would have been used to manufacture the:

   (i) Handle.   1

   _____

   (ii) Packaging.   1

   _____

   (c) Die casting can be used to manufacture products or component parts.

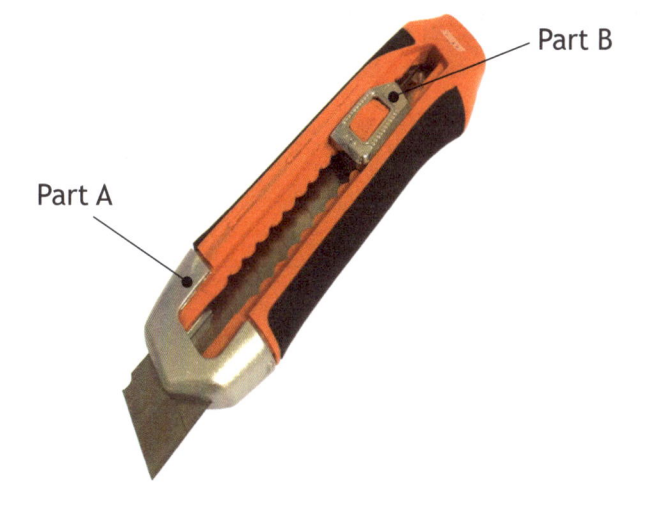

   Part A
   Part B

   State **two** features that would clearly identify that parts A and B have been die cast.   2

   _____

   _____

   [Turn over

9. 3D printers and laser cutters are widely used in the design and manufacture of products.

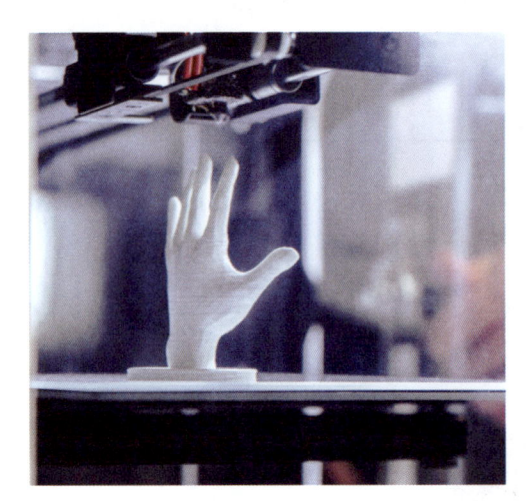

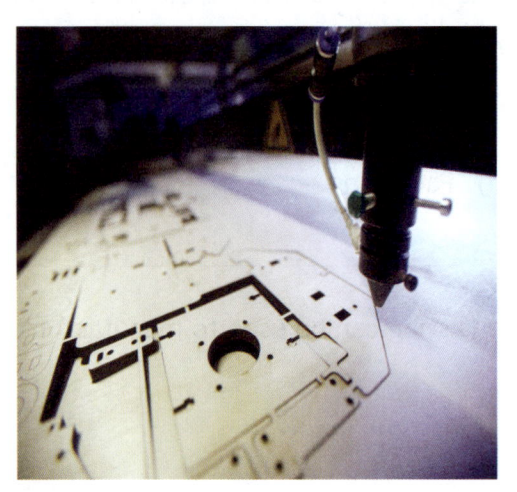

    (a) Describe the benefits of using 3D printers and laser cutters to design and mass produce products. **4**

    (b) Describe the impact that the use of these technologies has had on society. **2**

10. Products are being designed to be more sustainable.

Describe the steps designers and manufacturers can take to make products more sustainable. **3**

11. The bearings used in fidget spinners are standard components.

Bearing

Describe the benefits of using standard components in products. **3**

[END OF QUESTION PAPER]

ADDITIONAL SPACE FOR ANSWERS

NATIONAL 5
Answers

ANSWERS FOR

SQA NATIONAL 5 DESIGN AND MANUFACTURE 2018

NATIONAL 5 DESIGN AND MANUFACTURE 2017

SECTION 1

1. (a) (i) *An explanation similar to:*
    - Parts that are all the same
    - Parts supplied by a sub-contractor
    - Parts from an outside source
    - Parts that are mass produced
    - Parts that have multiple uses
    - Common tools fit them
    - Commonly used
    - Can be reused
    - **Any other suitable response**

    (ii) *One mark each for:*
    - You don't have to make them yourself
    - The parts will be made in large numbers so will be cheap to make
    - Consistency of accuracy
    - Consistency of quality (finish)
    - Quality assured
    - Easy to obtain
    - Saves time as no manufacturing is needed
    - No specialist tools required
    - Minimal skill required
    - Can use them in a range of products
    - **Any other suitable response**

   (b) (i) *A description that covers one of the following:*
    - Helps to keep the board flat
    - Won't warp
    - Won't twist
    - Edge of board protected from damage
    - Allows a wide board to be produced
    - Holds the board securely
    - Pulls strips together over their length
    - **Any other suitable response**

    (ii) *A description that covers two of the following:*
    - Softwood trees grow quickly and are therefore sustainable/hardwood trees grow slowly and are therefore less sustainable
    - Wood should be sourced from managed forests
    - Using tropical hardwoods endangers rainforests
    - Locally sourced
    - Lifespan of wood
    - Recyclability of chosen wood
    - **Any other suitable response**

   (c) (i) *A description that covers two of the following:*
    - Does the DVD fit into position
    - Can the DVDs be easily accessed
    - How many DVDs can be held
    - Does it hold DVDs securely
    - Are the pegs long enough
    - Are the pegs strong enough
    - Is the hole for the peg deep enough to ensure strength
    - Does it hold the weight of a DVD
    - **Any other suitable response**

    (ii) *One mark for:*
    - Cheaper than solid timber
    - Easy to work with
    - Sturdy (resistant) enough for purpose of model
    - Available in wide boards
    - **Any other suitable response**

   (d) *A description that covers two of the following:*
    - Quicker than repeated marking out
    - Accurate
    - Identical
    - Easier than traditional marking out methods
    - **Any other suitable response**

   (e) (i) *A description, referring to tools/processes, that covers two of the following:*
    - Cut the curve using a suitable named saw
    - External/internal curves machine sanded/sander
    - File/surform/rasp edges
    - Hand sand
    - **Any other suitable response**

    (ii) *A description of marking out and cutting, referring to tools/processes, that includes four of the following:*
    - Marking out two parallel lines
    - Marking out required depth
    - Cutting slot between the two parallel lines (reference must be made to tenon/gent's saw)
    - Remove waste material (naming a specific type of chisel is not required)
    - Levelling the slot to a consistent depth
    - **Any other suitable response**

    (iii) *A description, referring to tools/processes, that includes two of the following:*
    - Remove pencil marks/blemishes with sandpaper or eraser
    - Sand using rough sandpaper
    - Sand using smooth sandpaper
    - Wet the wood to raise the grain
    - **Any other suitable response**

    (iv) *One mark for:*
    - Looks better
    - Lasts longer/protects surface
    - **Any other suitable response**

   (f) *A description, referring to tools/processes that includes two of the following:*
    - Clamping to hold in position
    - Shaping corners
    - Cross file edges to shape
    - Draw file edges smooth
    - Smooth edges with abrasive paper
    - Polish edges
    - Drill holes
    - Countersink holes
    - Heat using strip heater/oven
    - Bend to shape
    - Secure in position to cool
    - **Any other suitable response**

SECTION 2

2. (a) *Candidates should describe four aesthetic aspects within the following broad areas:*
   - Colour
   - Shape
   - Form
   - Texture
   - Line
   - Proportion
   - Symmetry
   - Contrast
   - Pattern
   - Fashion
   - **Any other suitable response**

   (b) *To gain marks, candidates must describe the relationship between the ergonomic consideration and the part of this type of product.*
   A description that refers to six of the following:

   Anthropometric issues:
   - Chair seat width
   - Seat height increased to clear stairs
   - Longer back length to support baby
   - Adjustability of parts of the pram e.g. restraint straps/handles/seat angle
   - Hand grip

   Physiological issues:
   - Weight of chair
   - Strength of user
   - Comfort of user
   - Buttons for adjusting straps/heights of pram
   - Ease of folding/unfolding
   - Accessing areas of the pram

   Psychological issues:
   - Confidence issues surrounding user
   - Stability of chair
   - Belt for safety
   - High resolution colours used
   - Construction looks robust
   - Simplicity of use
   - Signalling of interactive components
   - **Any other suitable response**

3. (a) *One mark for:*
   - Cheaper than fully assembled furniture
   - Uses less storage space therefore readily available
   - Consumer can transport flat pack easily
   - Satisfaction of self-assembly
   - **Any other suitable response**

   (b) *A description that includes two of the following:*
   - Can stay ahead of the competition/adapt designs/new designs
   - Allows new shapes/less joining techniques to be used
   - Reduces unit costs
   - Reduces labour costs
   - Time efficient (man hours)
   - Reduces material used
   - Quicker production than traditional methods
   - Accurate
   - Can facilitate rapid prototyping
   - Easy to modify CAD file
   - Can be sent electronically
   - Physical storage minimised
   - Lots can be made at once
   - **Any other suitable response**

   (c) *Candidates may describe one of the following techniques via the use of text and/or graphics:*
   - Morphological Analysis
   - Brainstorming
   - Technology Transfer
   - Analogy
   - Lateral Thinking
   - Mood board
   - Lifestyle board
   - Take your pencil for a walk
   - Design Stories
   - SAM
   - Gathering public opinion through a market survey
   - Existing product board

   Example answer:
   Brainstorming
   The team will sit together and note down all of the ideas each person has, no matter how silly they seem. Some ideas may spark off thoughts in others, allowing different suggestions to be explored in the hope of coming up with a new idea.

4. (a) (i) *State any two of the following:*
   - Purchase of machinery
   - Associated computer hardware costs
   - Manufacture of mould/tooling
   - Training of workforce
   - **Any other suitable response**

   (ii) Process:
   - Injection moulding

   Justification:
   - Economies of scale/mass produced product
   - Low cost raw material
   - Intricate detail
   - High volume over short time periods
   - Reliable, established technology
   - **Any other suitable response**

   (iii) *One mark each for:*
   - Can be reheated and reshaped
   - Moulds easily
   - Readily available
   - Strong/robust
   - Hardwearing/durable
   - Available in a range of colours
   - Scratch resistant
   - In-built finish
   - Can be recycled
   - Easy to clean
   - Low cost bulk buying of raw material
   - Lightweight
   - **Any other suitable response**

   (iv) *One mark for:*
   - Polypropylene
   - HDPE
   - HIPS
   - PS
   - **Any other suitable response**

   (b) *One mark for:*
   - It is safe to use
   - It has been tested for safety
   - Ensures the product meets a minimum safety standard
   - To signify conformance with European Union regulations regarding product safety
   - Conforms to European environmental regulations
   - Shows sustainability in manufacturing
   - **Any other suitable response**

5. (a) (i) *A description that refers to a:*
- User trial
Example answer: Ask a range of people to run with the shoes over a variety of surfaces then provide feedback on how well they felt the shoe performed.

(ii) *A description that refers to one of the following:*
- Product comparison (this term scores one mark on its own)
- Survey
- Extended user trial
- Any other suitable response

(b) *One mark each for:*
- BOGOF
- Adverts, e.g. TV, radio, billboard, posters/leaflets
- Celebrity endorsement
- Free gifts/prizes, win a holiday
- Sell shoes under a big brand name
- Any other suitable response

(c) *One mark each for:*
- 2D graphic techniques
- 3D graphic techniques
- 3D solid model/CAD model/inventor (any named modelling package)
- Orthographic drawings/Dimensioned views/Working drawing
- Scaled up detail
- Exploded/assembly drawing
- Any other suitable response

(d) *A description that refers to two of the following:*
- See it in 3D (see what it looks like)/show it to others
- Provides an accurate representation of the sole
- Cheaper than traditional methods
- Time efficient (man hours)
- Changes can be easily made
- Problems can be identified at an early stage
- Alternative solutions can be made
- Very little waste material
- Any other suitable response

(e) (i) *One mark for:*
- Increased profits
- Low running costs
- Cheap material costs
- Skilled work force
- Cheap premises cost
- Cheap labour costs
- Any other suitable response

(ii) *One mark for:*
- Workers to be paid a living wage
- Acceptable health and safety at work conditions
- Respect the cultural identity/language of the workforce
- Any other suitable response

NATIONAL 5 DESIGN AND MANUFACTURE 2017 SPECIMEN QUESTION PAPER

SECTION 1

1. (a) (i) *Name any one of the following:*
- mahogany
- teak
- sapele
- cherry
- walnut
- Any other suitable response

(ii) *Name any one of the following:*
- brass
- bronze

(b) *Outline any two safety checks on the wood lathe.*
- blank centred
- blank secured between centres
- tool rest secure
- tool rest at correct height
- clearance between tool rest and blank

(c) (i) *A description and/or sketch of marking out and removing the corners, that refers to four of the following:*
- using a rule to draw diagonal lines to find centre on the ends of work piece
- using a set of compasses to draw circle/construct octagon
- using marking gauge to mark out corners to be removed
- holding work piece in bench vice when removing corners
- using smoothing plane to remove corners
- using centre punch to mark centres at both ends of the blank

(ii) Parting tool

(iii) *Name any one of the following:*
- outside callipers
- vernier callipers

(d) (i) *Description and/or sketch of how to cut out the notches identified with workshop tools. Typical responses are likely to include reference to:*
- cutting parallel lines with a tenon saw or jig saw.
- removing waste with a jig saw or bevel-edged chisel

(ii) *Name any one of the following:*
- Forstner drill
- hole saw

(e) (i) An explanation that includes two of the following reasons:
- accurate repeatability as you are drawing around the same template
- saves time as the complex shape only has to be drawn once
- complex curves would be difficult to mark out with marking out tools
- efficient positioning on material will reduce waste
- if a mistake is made while cutting it can be marked out again quickly
- can be used to check accuracy of parts once they have been cut out

(ii) Coping saw

(f) (i) Engineer's vice

(ii) *Name any one of the following:*
- Hacksaw
- Junior hacksaw

(iii) *State any three of the following:*
- Face-off
- Parallel turn
- Step turn
- Chamfer

(g) (i) *An explanation that includes any one of the following:*
- improves accuracy as the centre drill does not flex or move when drilling
- stopping twist drill from wandering off centre as the centre drill creates a small counter-sunk hole

(ii) *Name any one of the following:*
- Split die
- Die

(iii) *A description that includes two of the following:*
- use of cutting compound
- accurate alignment
- chamfering the end
- half turn forward, quarter turn back
- adjusting the split die

(h) (i) *State any two of the following:*
- translucent — suited to emitting light
- can be formed into shape required
- heat resistant to 200 degrees
- polishes well
- rigid, holds it shape
- can be drilled and cut to shape required
- **Any other suitable response**

(ii) Strip heater

(iii) *An explanation that includes any two of the following:*
- it will be quicker because it is easier to finish the flat edges before the shade is formed
- it will be quicker and easier because there are fewer corners and awkward parts to finish
- it is simpler to hold and clamp when it is a flat shape
- the acrylic is less likely to snap because it can be held securely

2. (a) (i) *Outline must reference information gained from a user trip, ie gained from personal experience. Outline of any of the following:*
- ease of use
- how it works
- how it performs on different surfaces
- how long it takes to charge
- important design features
- areas for improvement
- ease of maintenance
- **Any other suitable response**

(ii) *Outline must reference information gained from a questionnaire, ie gained from sources other than personal use. Outline of any of the following:*
- opinions on aesthetic appeal
- opinions on price
- age of the user
- where it is most likely to be used
- likes and dislikes
- **Any other suitable response**

(b) A description of the key stages of a **user trip** or **questionnaire** that includes any three of the following:

Typical responses for a **user trip** could include reference to:
- preparation — plan the user trip, consider purpose of user trip, what information is required from the user trip, read instruction and find out how to use product, identify important stages in using the product, eg install, use and storage
- undertaking — use at each stage, eg unpacking and installing, use, maintenance storage. Use in all possible conditions and environments
- collating — record and analyse information from user trip

Typical responses for a **questionnaire** could include reference to:
- preparation — consider the target market when wording questions, identify what information is required, write and trial questions, amend question after trial if required
- conducting — make sure target mark answers the questionnaire. Ensure questionnaires are completed and returned on time, ensure sufficient questionnaires have been completed
- collating — record and analyse information from questionnaire

(c) *A description that includes two of the following:*
- provides direction to exploration and refinement
- improves decision making as a result of evaluation against specification
- allows most promising ideas to be identified/taken forward
- identifies important factors to consider in the development and refinement

3. *Description of the key stages of brainstorming or morphological analysis that includes any three of the following:*

Typical responses for **brainstorming** could include reference to:
- planning — identify the purpose of the brainstorming session, consider the size of the group, invite suitable people to take part
- conducting — get group to rephrase the question, have a warm-up session, establish rules, set a time limit, avoid moments of silence and maintain momentum, record every thought
- summary — discuss most unusual ideas, disregard weakest ideas, and identify most promising ideas

Typical responses for **morphological analysis** could include reference to:
- planning — analysis of problem/product, identify factors that will be/are important to solving the problem or improving the product, generate a range of different options for each factor, produce a matrix
- using — randomly or systematically select an option from each factor to produce different alternatives
- summary — disregard weakest ideas, and identify most promising ideas

4. (a) *Explanation including any two of the following:*
- sketches can be produced quickly which allows lots of ideas to be produced in a short time
- you are not limited or constrained by computer software
- as sketches are quick to produce they can be changed, altered or discarded

- you do not need any specific information, ideas can emerge naturally
- **Any other suitable response**

(b) *Description must include two of the following:*
- allows information to be communicated to production team
- allows dimensions in order to provide cutting lists
- communicates construction details of different component parts
- can be used to work out costings
- helps planning for manufacture
- **Any other suitable response**

5. (a) *Outline two reasons from the following:*
- physical interaction gives feedback on ergonomics
- it can be given to others to test and evaluate
- can be altered and refined as feedback is gained
- provides better understanding of 3D form
- provides better understanding of faults and how to improve them

(b) *Outline two reasons from the following:*
- good detail and clarity will impress the client
- improves presentation as different views and versions can be created once the original model has been created
- can be rotated and animated which could provide clarity to the client
- can be used in video conferencing/virtual presentations
- can be produced and altered quickly which means changes could be made during presentation with client
- accurate representation of materials and textures will improve communication with client

6. (a) *Description must reference how anthropometrics may have influenced the trike. Typical responses could include reference to four of the following:*
- position of pedals in relation to leg length
- height of seat in relation to popliteal height
- height of crossbar in relation to leg length
- size of seat in relation to hip width
- position of handle bars in relation to reach
- diameter of handle bars in relation to grip
- width of handle bars in relation to shoulder width
- length of grips in relation to hand width
- **Any other suitable response**

(b) (i) *Outline two reasons from the following:*
- bright
- colourful
- friendly
- fun
- **Any other suitable response**

(ii) *Outline two reasons from the following:*
- safety
- price
- stability
- easy to use
- ease of maintenance
- durability
- **Any other suitable response**

7. (a) *A description that includes two of the following:*
- research into new materials pushes the development on new products
- research into new technology pushes the development on new products
- research into new production methods pushes the development on new products
- innovative technology generates new products
- new products are created that are not based on market research

(b) *A description that includes two of the following:*
- established name
- reputation
- guaranteed sales
- ease of advertising
- premium pricing
- customer loyalty

SECTION 2

8. (a) (i) *Select a suitable material:*
- acrylic

An explanation that includes one of the following:
- clear – see through to make things easier to measure
- durable – gets used a lot and should not wear easily
- hard – provides a good edge for drawing
- impact resistant – rulers get dropped and misused
- suitable for injection moulding
- **Any other suitable response**

(ii) *Select a suitable material:*
- polypropylene

An explanation that include one of the following:
- impact resistant – lid gets bashed and dropped
- flexible – live hinge on lid, instruments get pushed into lid
- transparent – can see contents
- scratch resistant – gets put in and out of bag and could get scratched
- suitable for injection moulding
- **Any other suitable response**

(b) (i) *One mark for:*
- reduces stress
- stops thinning
- retains material thickness
- reduces risk of insert sticking to the pattern

(ii) *One mark for:*
- ensures no air is trapped in corners
- ensures vacuum is created in internal parts of the insert
- ensures internal corners are formed accurately

(iii) *One mark for:*
- reduces risk of plastic sticking to the pattern
- ease of removing the pattern

(c) *State any two of the following:*
- injection marks
- ejection marks
- flashing
- good surface finish
- accuracy
- complexity

(d) Die casting

9. *One mark each for any two of the following:*
- reduces work force as work is automated
- reduces lead time as less tooling is required
- increased efficiency as machines can run 24 hours a day
- speeds up production as tools run at a higher speed
- flexibility as machines can be programmed to do different tasks

- is suitable for small production runs as less tooling is required
- provides consistency as each part is manufactured identically
- Any other suitable response

10. *To gain full marks, benefits to both consumer and manufacturer must be described. Description of benefits of knock-down fittings to the **consumer**, including any of the following:*
    - as the furniture is supplied unassembled (flat pack), the furniture can be transported from the shop or manufacturer easily
    - consumers can take their goods home on the day and do not have to plan or pay for delivery
    - reduction in manufacturing costs can be passed on to the consumer making furniture more affordable
    - furniture can be assembled in situ allowing large pieces of furniture to be fitted into smaller spaces
    - no requirement for tools or equipment as tools are supplied with flat pack furniture
    - Any other suitable response

    Description of benefits of knock-down fittings to the manufacturer *including any of the following:*
    - reduces the cost of production
    - reduced need for skilled workforce
    - increased use of automation as parts and assembly can be simplified
    - no requirement to assemble product
    - less stages in a product's manufacture
    - easier to quality control
    - Any other suitable response

11. (a) *A description of one benefit of manufacturing technologies on the workforce that includes one of the following:*
    - highly trained workforce
    - transferable skills
    - safer working environment
    - improved working conditions
    - Any other suitable response

    A description of one drawback of manufacturing technologies on the workforce that includes one of the following:
    - reduction in workforce
    - deskilling of workforce
    - loss of traditional skills
    - Any other suitable response

    (b) *A description that includes three of the following:*
    - pollution
    - waste
    - sustainability
    - recycling

NATIONAL 5 DESIGN AND MANUFACTURE 2018

SECTION 1

1. (a) (i) *Name any one alternative softwood:*
   - Spruce
   - Cedar
   - Douglas fir
   - Larch
   - Scots/Piranha pine (not 'pine')
   - Any other suitable response

   (ii) *One mark for each valid description and/or sketch, up to a maximum of two marks:*
   - Marking out a joint
   - Drilling an appropriate joint
   - Applying glue to the edges of the pieces of softwood
   - Clamping the glued pieces together
   - Any other suitable response

   (b) (i) Forstner bit.

   (ii) *Name one of the following:*
   - Twist drill.
   - Jobber drill.

   (iii) *Name any one of the following:*
   - Disc sander
   - Belt sander
   - Scroll saw
   - Fret saw
   - Band saw
   - Orbital sander
   - Jig saw
   - Any other suitable response

   (iv) *One mark for correct response that includes the following:*
   - The flush surface prevents scratches from the screw heads

   (c) (i) Bradawl

   (ii) One mark for correct response:
   - Coping saw
   - Abrafile
   - Any other suitable response

   (iii) *An explanation that includes **two** of the following reasons:*
   - Wax can be applied quickly using a cloth rather than a brush
   - Cleaning up is easier as no washing of a brush is required
   - Less chance of runs as wax is more viscous than varnish
   - Wax gives a smooth finish whereas varnish can feel rough
   - Wax gives an instant dry finish, while varnish takes a longer time to dry
   - Gives an alternative aesthetic quality
   - Any other suitable response

   (d) *A description and/or sketch of **both** marking out and cutting, that could include some of the following. Maximum three marks may be awarded to responses that refer to only one of the stages:*

   Marking out stage
   - Mark position of joint on top surface with rule and pencil
   - Draw lines at 90 degrees with try square
   - Mark depth with marking gauge

ANSWERS FOR NATIONAL 5 DESIGN AND MANUFACTURE

Cutting stage
- Use a G-clamp to hold a guide piece of wood next to the line
- Cut the two lines to the required depth with a **tenon saw/gent's saw**
- Remove the waste wood with a chisel (naming a specific chisel is not required)
- Level the bottom of the joint with a hand router/chisel
- Any other suitable response

(e) (i) *One mark for each correct response:* 3
  A — taper turning/chamfering
  B — step turning/parallel turning
  C — knurling

(ii) *Statement of two of the following adjustments, with one mark for each correct response:* 2
  - Change the tool
  - Reduce the spindle speed
  - Change the speed
  - Change the angle of the compound slide
  - Any other suitable response

(f) (i) *An explanation that includes two of the following, with one mark for each correct response:*
  - To create a 3D form so that it is more accurate
  - To make sure the bowls are identical
  - Quicker when making more than one
  - Any other suitable response

(ii) *One mark for correct response, which may include:*
  - Oven
  - Thermoforming centre
  - Vacuum former
  - Any other suitable response

(iii) *One mark for correct response, which may include:*
  - Scroll saw
  - Fret saw
  - Band saw
  - Jig saw
  - Hegner saw
  - Any other suitable response

(iv) *A description that includes two of the following stages in the correct order, with one mark from each bullet point to a maximum of two:*
  - Filing/scraping
  - Use abrasive papers/cloth/wool
  - Polishing/buffing
  - Any other suitable response

(g) (i) *One mark for correct response:*
  - Aluminium
  - Tin
  - Zinc
  - Any other suitable response

(ii) Odd-leg callipers.

(iii) Engineers square.

(iv) *Name any one of the following:*
  - Tin snips
  - Junior hacksaw
  - Hacksaw
  - Cold chisel
  - Notcher/guillotine
  - Coping saw
  - Any other suitable response

2. (a) *One mark for each valid point leading to a clear explanation, up to a maximum of two marks. Explanation must reference benefits of using a questionnaire:*
   - A wide range of people can be sampled
   - Can be collated quickly
   - Specific questions can be asked e.g. aesthetics, ergonomics, function – to direct the person being surveyed
   - Can be written to suit the target market
   - A rating system can be used to further refine the process
   - The results are easy to present in the form of graphs/charts
   - Any other suitable response

   (b) *One mark for each valid description up to a maximum of two marks. Description must reference the use of a specification in the design process:*
   - To give guidance during the design process
   - As an ongoing evaluation tool
   - Any other suitable response

3. (a) *One mark for correct response up to a maximum of three marks. A description, or drawing of a morphological analysis table, that refers to the following stages:*
   - Identify a set of suitable parameters for the table heading
   - Populate the rows with suitable attributes
   - Choose combinations of attributes
   - Generate ideas from results
   - Any other suitable response

   (b) *One mark for correct response, which may include the following:*
   - Brainstorming
   - Taking your pencil for a walk
   - Thought showers
   - Technology transfer
   - Analogy/biomimicry
   - Lateral thinking
   - SCAMPER
   - Any other suitable response

4. *One mark for each valid point leading to a clear description up to a maximum of three marks:*
   - Alignment of parts prior to assembly can be communicated
   - It is easy to gain a quick visual indication of the number of parts
   - A fully rendered model can be used to evaluate aesthetics
   - The concept can be sent electronically very quickly
   - Alterations can be made very quickly
   - The model can be orientated to different angles
   - A machining file can be generated from the model
   - Suitable to show to client
   - Doesn't use materials like a physical model
   - Any other suitable response

5. (a) *One mark for each valid explanation up to a total of two marks. The explanation must refer to the development of the blender, and include two of the following reasons:*
   - Sizes and proportions can be quickly checked before developing further
   - Allows the user to interact with the blender and give feedback
   - Sketch models are quick to produce allowing a lot to be made in a shorter time
   - Any other suitable response

(b) *One mark for each valid explanation, which **must** refer to development of the blender, up to a total of two marks. Answers from 5(a) cannot be repeated. Explanation must include **two** of the following reasons:*
- The capacity of the bowl can be checked so that it can hold enough fruit/veg etc.
- Size of handle can be evaluated so that it fits the hand
- Size of dial can be evaluated to see if it fits the fingers
- Footprint on kitchen work surface can be seen easily to judge how much space would be required
- Checking that parts fit together
- Checking proportion of parts
- **Any other suitable response**

6. (a) (i) *One mark for each valid point leading to a clear description up to a maximum of **two** marks. Description must reference how the function of **one or both** of the backpacks have been influenced by the target market:*

    Backpack A
    Typical responses could include reference to:
    - Can store commonly used walking/climbing equipment
    - Includes lots of compartments to organise equipment
    - The lightweight material makes the backpack easy to carry in the hills
    - The straps are adjustable to suit different users
    - The colour is bright meaning that the user is easily seen outdoors
    - The fabric is easy to clean if it gets dirty in the hills
    - **Any other suitable response**

    Backpack B
    Typical responses could include reference to:
    - The backpack is small so easy to carry for a child
    - There are separate sections for items like pencils, water bottle etc.
    - The backpack material is resistant to spills/will not stain
    - **Any other suitable response**

    (ii) *One mark for each valid point leading to a clear description up to a maximum of two marks. Description must reference how the aesthetics of **one or both** of the backpacks have been influenced by the target market:*

    Backpack A
    Typical responses could include reference to:
    - The contrast of the orange and grey colours would appeal to an adult consumer
    - The target market may associate a sense of weight/balance provided by the use of black at the bottom of the backpack
    - The bright colour will make the backpack stand out in the hills

    Backpack B
    Typical responses could include reference to:
    - The animal theme appeals to children
    - The bright pink colour may appeal to children
    - Children would be attracted by the shiny surface of the material
    - **Any other suitable response**

(b) *One mark for each technique stated up to a maximum of two marks. State **two** of the following marketing techniques:*
- Introductory offers
- Free gifts
- Celebrity endorsement
- Adverts
- Sell under brand name
- Reviews
- **Any other suitable response**

7. (a) *One mark for each valid point leading to a clear description up to a maximum of four marks. Description must reference how ergonomics may have influenced the camera. Typical responses could refer to:*
- The size of the handle to fit the hand
- The size of the button to fit the finger
- The weight of the camera so that it is easy for a child to support
- How hard you need to press the button
- Can you see clearly through the view finder/see the screen easily
- Is the layout of the control features easy to understand?
- **Any other suitable response**

(b) *One mark for each valid point leading to a clear description up to a maximum of two marks. Description must reference how performance may have influenced the camera. Typical responses could refer to:*
- Maintenance
- Life expectancy
- Fitness-for-purpose
- Safety
- Changing batteries
- Withstanding misuse
- Easy to clean
- Value for money

(c) *One mark for each description up to a maximum of two marks. Description must include two ways in which research into new materials pushes development on new products:*
- Research into new technology pushes the development on new products
- Research into new production methods pushes the development on new products
- Innovative technology generates new products
- New products are created that are not based on market research
- **Any other suitable response**

SECTION 2

8. (a) (i) *One mark for naming a suitable thermoplastic:*
    - Polypropylene (or PP)
    - ABS
    - Polystyrene (HIPS)
    - Nylon
    - Cellulose Acetate
    - HDPE
    - uPVC
    - Polycarbonate

    One mark for a valid point explaining its suitability. Typical responses could refer to:
    - Impact resistant — knife gets bashed and dropped

ANSWERS FOR NATIONAL 5 DESIGN AND MANUFACTURE

- Durable – resists wear of moving parts
- Does not snap easily – will resist being pushed when cutting
- Can be coloured to suit user preference
- Scratch resistant – could be put in and out of tool box etc
- **Any other suitable response**

(ii) *To gain marks, it is not possible to repeat from section (i). One mark for naming a suitable thermoplastic:*
- Polystyrene (HIPS)
- ABS
- Polypropylene (or PP)
- PVC
- Nylon
- Cellulose Acetate
- HDPE
- LDPE
- uPVC
- PE/Polythene
- PET
- Polycarbonate

One mark for a valid point explaining its suitability. Typical responses could refer to:
- Flexible – allows knife to be held in place
- Scratch resistant – makes packaging always look good
- Transparent – can see contents
- Available in sheet form so that it is easy to manufacture
- **Any other suitable response**

(b) (i) Injection moulding.

(ii) *One mark for correct process:*
- Vacuum forming
- Thermoforming
- **Any other suitable response**

(c) *One mark for each identification feature of die casting, up to a maximum of two marks:*
- Split lines
- Injection marks
- Ejection marks
- Flashing
- Good surface finish
- Accuracy
- Complexity
- **Any other suitable response**

9. (a) *Description of benefits of 3D printers and laser cutters including any of the following. One mark for each benefit up to a maximum of four marks:*

3D printers/Laser cutters
- Models can be made with no craft skills
- The process is fully automated
- No need for workshops
- Model can be created directly from cad drawing
- Creates complex models that are free from the restraints of traditional manufacturing techniques
- Accuracy of parts
- Reduces work force/wages as work is automated
- Increased efficiency as machines can run 24 hours a day
- Provides consistency as each part is manufactured identically

3D printer:
- Same or similar materials to the final product can be used

Laser cutter:
- Reduces lead time as less tooling is required
- Have a faster production rate than tradition methods
- **Any other suitable response**

(b) *One mark for each valid point leading to a clear description that includes two of the following, up to a maximum of two marks:*
- Fewer workers required
- Workers require a new skill set
- Lower salaries
- Economic decline of employee (or ex-employee) living area
- Processes are flexible in the manufacture of products
- The price of 3d printers has made them affordable for home use meaning people can manufacture their own replacement parts
- **Any other suitable response**

10. *One mark for each valid point leading to a clear description of the steps designers and manufacturers could take to make products more sustainable, up to a maximum of three marks:*
- Reduce
- Reuse
- Recycle
- Rethink
- Lifespan

Candidates can gain marks with multiple responses under each bullet point.

11. *One mark for each valid point leading to a clear description of benefits of using standard components, up to a maximum of three marks:*
- Produced in standard sizes so easy to incorporate into designs
- Reduces the need for skilled workforce
- Cheaper than producing yourself
- Can be used on different Products
- Reliable/quality assured by Producer
- Ease of repair/maintenance
- Available in large quantities/easy to source
- Will fit common tools
- Can transfer across different products
- Don't have to manufacture them yourself
- Fewer stages in production
- **Any other suitable response**

Acknowledgements

Permission has been sought from all relevant copyright holders and Hodder Gibson is grateful for the use of the following:

Image © Kitch Bain/stock.adobe.com (2017 page 10);
Image © ayzek/Shutterstock.com (2017 page 12);
Image © tankist276/stock.adobe.com (2017 page 14);
CE Mark © European Union, 1995–2018 (http://eur-lex.europa.eu/legal-content/EN/TXT/PDF/?uri=CELEX:32008R0765&from=EN) (2017 page 15);
The BSI Kitemark device is reproduced with kind permission of The British Standards Institution. This is a registered trademark in the United Kingdom and in certain other countries. Copyright © 2018 BSI. All rights reserved (2017 page 15);
Image © Engin Sezer/Shutterstock.com (2017 page 16);
Two images © Kaspars Grinvalds/Shutterstock.com (2017 SQP page 12);
Image © Murlakatum/Shutterstock.com (2017 SQP page 16);
Image © Carl Bertossi/stock.adobe.com (2017 SQP page 17);
Image of Helix pencil case with Helix materials is reproduced by kind permission of MapedHelix (2017 SQP page 20);
Image of Maped set of compasses is reproduced by kind permission of MapedHelix (2017 SQP page 22);
Image © Kzenon/stock.adobe.com (2017 SQP page 23);
Image © sergeyshibur/stock.adobe.com (2017 SQP page 24);
Image © kriangphoto31/stock.adobe.com (2017 SQP page 24);
Image © Monkey Business Images/stock.adobe.com (2017 SQP page 25);
Image © grafvision/Shutterstock.com (2018 page 11);
Image © M.studio/stock.adobe.com (2018 page 12);
Image © Sergey Mironov/Shutterstock.com (2018 page 13);
Image © Svetislav1944/Shutterstock.com (2018 page 13);
Image © RimDream/Shutterstock.com (2018 page 14);
Image © fotofabrika/stock.adobe.com (2018 page 18);
Image © Pressmaster/stock.adobe.com (2018 page 18);
Image © Rasdi Abdul Rahman/Shutterstock.com (2018 page 19).